There is oil deep under the ground. It is a dark, thick, sticky liquid.

This is an oil rig.

It pumps oil up from under the ground.

A well is drilled to get the oil out. The drill is long and thin, with big steel teeth.

At the top is a platform. Men live on the platform for some weeks.

They travel there and back in a helicopter.

Some platforms float on big tanks. Chains attach the rig to the ground.

chains

Some platforms have long legs that stand on the ground.

Derricks support the drill. They stand on top of the rigs.

This ship is an oil tanker.

It transports the oil.

We get lots of different things from oil.

Small amounts of oil are stored in oil drums.

This is a steel band.

The drums are all oil drums!